HOW

TO

BE HAPPY

How to Be Happy: A Guide to Experience the Church's Missing Commodity

Copyright © 2020 Eric William Gilmour

*Cover design by Brit Richards

ISBN: 172085565X

ISBN-13: 978-1720855651

HOW

TO

BE

HAPPY

A guide to experience the churches missing commodity.

Eric Gilmour

"And the disciples were continually filled with joy and with the Holy Spirit."

— ACTS 13:52

CONTENTS

FOREWORD

Throughout Eric and I's life, we seem to see the number 143 everywhere we go. The number has a lot of significance *for* us and *to* us. While I was in London in 2017, the Lord spoke to me out of Psalm 143, namely the eighth and ninth verse.

"Let me hear Your lovingkindness *in the morning*; For I trust in You; Teach me the way in which I should walk; For to You I lift up my soul. Deliver me, O Lord, from my enemies; *I take refuge in You.*" (Psalm 143:8-9 emphasis added)

I would encourage you, allow yourself to hear the lovingkindness of God in the *morning*. Allow Him to be the first acknowledgement of your day. In this, you'll find a satisfaction and a defense that nothing can compete with.

God becomes the refuge and defender of those who take solace in Him. Let Him be your shield and His joy will be make yours. He isn't an afterthought or a secondary option. He is the One we make first, and as we do, He becomes *for* us the Defender that He promises to be.

—BROOKE GILMOUR

INTRODUCTION

Before receiving a sermon, entering prayer, or even reading a book, I like to start with simply breathing in and breathing out. I would encourage you, as well, to simply *settle in* and *relax*. Why? Because rest is the *realm* of perception. It isn't merely taking deep breaths that opens our receptivity but the *relinquishing* of our own efforts. If you're going to receive anything from the Lord, it will come *only* by such means. The great Psalm instructed, "Be still, and know..." (Psalm 46:10 NIV).

Notice, the knowing is *in the stillness*. *This* stillness enables us to receive. It might not be common practice to take deep breaths before cracking open a book or even offering up prayer, yet this routine *paired* with forfeiting our human effort literally opens our receptors. If the things of God are released to us without intentional reception on our part, they'll just bounce off.

When our receptivity is maximized, that which we retain from the Lord is maximized, as well. Don't short circuit your experience of God by your own scattered mind and desire to make something happen. Just rest. This will always cause the soul to give up and give God His proper place.

INFUSION

"Joy isn't a mere possession, but a Person."

God wants to give you a *gift*. Of course, He wants to give many... but allow me to dial in this teaching on a specific gift. As I do, remember something about a gift: it has nothing to do with you. In other words, all you must do is receive. Your merit doesn't release it; His goodness does. There are no hoops to jump through or special requirements. Red tape isn't the language of the Kingdom.

To be specific, I feel that the Lord is releasing the gift of *joy* on the body of Christ, because it's so desperately needed. We have a serious joy famine on our hands... may this work remedy that. Many people deal with a *real* sense of heaviness. They become scattered in their minds. Excess *thinking* becomes normal. These things ought not be.

When we wait on the Lord, it pulls the Word to us. David said, "I wait for your word..." (Psalm 119:74). In other words, the *Word* comes through *waiting*. If we would take time to simply wait on Him, we would receive His Word. Why do people have no clue what God is saying? They simply won't *wait*. If the Word travels to me on the path of my own waiting... then I'll surely experience a famine of Word in my life if I allow busyness to eliminate the simple art of *waiting*.

Waiting is taking the time to give God all of your attention. It's a *turning* of your attention, if you will. Impatience is often the very thing that steals our attention and doesn't allow us to wait on the Lord. *Impatience is an idol factory*. If you don't want to wait on God and you decide to go do *something else,* you will absolutely fashion something else in His place. Remember when Moses went to the mountain and Israel became restless? They fashioned an idol in His place and they even named the idol "Yahweh."

You can name your idol whatever you'd like. You could name it something spiritual or positive sounding. At the end of the day, it's still an object that is wrongfully taking the place of God. It's simple: if the origin is off, the whole thing is off. If our hearts are producing a dark thing, we can't give it a pretty enough label to redeem it. If it counters the will of God for our attention to be fixed on Him, it isn't worthy of our focus.

"Impatience is an idol factory."

Impatience is disinterest in the Dove. Let me explain. Remember, Noah let the first bird out and then the second and he waited for the return of the *dove*. If we won't wait for the Dove (the Spirit), we become disinterested. We are more into our own plans. If our hearts aren't laid at His feet, they always try to take His seat. It's the human disposition to try to take His place.

However, when we wait upon Him, we give Him His proper throne in our hearts. If we choose not to wait and be still, we are actually saying, "I've got this. I don't need You to rule me. I'll go forward saying all the right things and sounding the part, but I don't need Your actual reign in my life."

The interesting thing is, if we lay at His fect, He actually calls us to sit with Him (see Ephesians 2:6).

Yet, if we try to be seated on the throne apart from Him, our attempt is futile.

"If our hearts aren't laid at His feet, they always try to take His seat."

A Kingdom Infusion

My friend David Popovici says, "Some of us don't have a new nature. We just have the old man and he just changed his clothes." If there is one thing that I'm seeing in my travels, it's this: the church is lacking *joy*. The Bible says, "The kingdom of God is not eating and drinking, but righteousness and peace and **joy** in the Holy Spirit" (Romans 14:17, emphasis added).

Joy is in the Kingdom! Dr. Gordon Fee, in his book *Paul, the People, and the Spirit of God,* said, "Joy is the hallmark of genuine spirituality." In other words, if there is really a flow from the vine to the branch, the fruit that will come out as a result is joy. You can bank on joy when you touch God. God brings His realm with Him when He comes. His nature is joy. When He is allowed in, He dispenses His Person *into* you. In this, joy becomes a part of you and it's no longer dependent upon circumstances around you, but the God who is in you.

In this mode of receiving, your joy can't be touched by *anything* in the natural, for your joy is rooted in the vine. I want to tell you, a lack of joy is a lack of life! I was on Anna Maria Island and the Lord told me something very interesting. He said, "I'm going to change everything about you."

I got away by myself and entered a small prayer chapel to give my attention to Him. I became quiet *and* still before the Lord. Notice both the quietness and the stillness. Quietness is the absence of external noise. Stillness is the absence of internal noise. So many people become quiet in their surroundings but are filled with noise internally, thus they have no stillness. This is key, because our instruction is not to merely be quiet, but to *be still*. What we really need in order to hear the Lord is to remove ourselves from the hurricane outside and to remove the hurricane on the inside!

As I sat in quietness and stillness in the chapel, I felt the Lord speak something to me. I actually saw in a flash the R&B group called *112* out of the blue. I remembered them and thought, "Whoa, the Lord must be saying something to me." I instantly remembered Joel 1:12 which says, "The people's joy is withered away" (NIV). I've found that the majority of Christians whom my wife and I know have no joy whatsoever. They may have lots of "revelation," but no joy. They might have a big ministry and they might have it together on the outside, but totally lack genuine *joy* on the inside.

Andrew Murray said, "If the hands on the clock are not ticking, you know there is an internal problem." Likewise, if joy is not present in the life of a believer, you know there is an internal problem. Obviously, there is an attack in this area in the body of Christ. The attack isn't necessarily on joy itself, but it's an attack on our *connection to the vine!* The evidence of your connection being attacked is a lack of joy. Your joy levels can be used as a measuring stick for your connection with Jesus!

Let me just clear the air... *God wants you to be happy!* All my life, I've heard different things than that. I've heard that God is not interested in my happiness. I've now learned that He wants me to be so happy, not in stuff and things, but in Him. He wants me to be happy in my reality! So often, people are caught placing their happiness in unreality.

"But when He, the Spirit of truth, comes..." (John 16:13). The translation for the word *truth* in this passage is actually the word *reality* in the original text. "When He, the Spirit of reality, comes..."

He shows us what is *real* and what is *not real*. So many can't decide what's real and what's fake. The Holy Spirit enables us to decipher the difference. What is real to God? It's the thing that lasts forever! What's real to Him is that which comes from Him, lasts forever, and never began! That is reality to God. The Spirit of *reality* has come to show you what is real... what came from God, what lasts forever, and what has no beginning! He came to show us the eternality of God, if you will.

It doesn't get anymore real than the fact that a connection to the joyful vine cannot produce anything but a joyful branch. Our beings haven't come into distance contact with a joyful King but have literally been infused with His joyful Spirit. This isn't just demeanor-altering truth but nature altering reality.

2

JOYFUL FEAR

"The fear of the Lord yields a return called joy."

The fear of the Lord opens up a happiness within us. It's actually the key! Many are so confused about what the fear of the Lord is. There is endless teaching about what it is and what it isn't. One day, my understanding on this subject became clear! It hit me like a ton of bricks. The fear of the Lord is best understood by examining the first time it's mentioned in the Bible! It's in Genesis 22 when Abraham took Isaac onto the mountain to sacrifice him. Everything was in place and ready. Abraham lifted his knife to kill his only son and God stopped the process. What did God say to Abraham? "For now I know that you fear God since you have not withheld your son, your only son, from me" (Genesis 22:12). Abraham didn't allow even the most precious and promised things to take the place of God. I pray that God would expose the things that have taken His place and revive our gaze upon His face!

May we get back to hitting the bull's-eye, which is intimacy with Him. In this, we will experience the sap that drips from His person and walk in the life He has ordained with joy unspeakable and full of glory! A lack of the fear of the Lord has absolutely robbed our joy. You might say, "Well, because I am unhappy, are you saying I don't fear God?" No! What I am saying is that in any area where you've let something block your gaze on the Lord, it is blocking the *fear of the Lord.*

When the fear of the Lord is blocked, you can't find true happiness. The fear of the Lord is a posture that decrees, "Lord, You are number one! You are the only thing that matters. You are all that I need."

Fear and joy are rarely used in the same sentence. The kingdom has a means of functioning that often defies logic, ultimately bringing about a supernatural result. The path to joy being fear isn't a formula we often dwell on, yet we ought to. A holy fear of God results in bearing fruit.

Not merely the fruit of holiness, righteous living, and reverence but the joyful fun that God Himself enjoys! This *fear of God* isn't a trivial power-play on the part of God but a means by which He can shed abroad the blessing of joy on His people. Let this be your mainstay and your default!

3

THE GREATEST GIFT OF ALL

"The best present is always presence."

Peple get happy when they get gifts. It's just true. Likewise, God instills happiness in us when He offers us gifts. Don't ever allow yourself to be condemned for enjoying that which the Lord has provided. Paul said that God "richly supplies us with all things to enjoy" (1 Timothy 6:17).

The angel came to Mary and said, "Do not be afraid; for behold, I bring you good news of great joy which will be for all the people" (Luke 2:10). What brought joy? A gift named Jesus. People lack joy when they want something more than what they have already been given. What does that mean? God has given you His actual Person... the greatest riches that we could obtain. When people want something *more* than what's already here, they cut off their ability to be *happy*.

When in prayer, I simply cease my *thinking* and allow my heart to go up to Him in worship. I begin to drink of the Lord. He Himself said, "If anyone is thirsty, let him come to Me and drink" (John 7:37). He isn't offering something apart from Himself. He Himself is *in the cup*.

We drink of His own Person. Folks wonder how to drink of Him in prayer. It's simple: *less thinking, more drinking*. Our minds can hinder us from receiving in the prayer closet more than we might think. You can drink of Him in public, in private, listening to a message, on the job, or anywhere else.

"...less thinking, more drinking."

I remember working construction one time and feeling so bogged down by life. It was so hot outside physically. I was strapped financially. I was struggling with people relationally. I was oppressed atmospherically. I was surrounded by crude men who would blast profane music and talk about having casual sex with different women. Nothing about my situation looked spiritual. Yet, I would break away and find a place of prayer. The only place I could find was an outdoor port-a-potty on the job site. Pornography was plastered all over the inside of the portable restroom. I would close my eyes and lift my hands and I would begin to drink of the Lord. That hot, disgusting outdoor bathroom would suddenly be filled with the glory of God. Even though it was still hot and still stunk, it didn't matter to me. The surroundings were irrelevant to me when He showed up. When I would leave the restroom to return to work, I suddenly felt untouchable. I felt I was removed from under the influence of the vulgar men I was working with!

The Irreplaceable Approach

I was once walking with my wife in heavy rain and I said to her, "Babe, I know where a pavilion is!" She said to me plainly, "Great. Then take me there." In other words, the knowledge of the pavilion being there was not the same as running under it. In the same way, knowing that Jesus is joy is not the same as actually drinking Him. Knowing that He is drinkable isn't the same as actually drinking Him. You can't hide behind theology or anything else.

You must simply approach Him. Jesus won't share His throne with a theology or a doctrine. He wants to sit there personally and *actually*... not just theologically.

> *"Jesus won't share His throne with a theology or a doctrine."*

Often what stops us from drinking deep is thinking deep. We focus so much on what this person says or what that person thinks and it hinders us from simply drinking of the Lord fully. It's time to not give a rip about the opinions of those around us, but simply place the chalice of God to our lips and allow Him in.

I was once in the closet drinking of Him, and as I did, I slipped into a vision. In the vision, Jesus had a *massive* paintbrush dripping with red paint. He was dragging it behind Him and walking toward me. I am looking at Him, unsure of what He is about to do to me. Suddenly, He took this massive paintbrush and smeared it across my face and painted a big smile on my face. He then grabbed me and brought me face-to-face with Him and said, "Happily enjoy all the details of your life!" This changed me forever! He wants to anoint you with the oil of gladness!

He wants to put upon you the oil of joy so that through face-to-face contact with Him, you can enjoy every aspect of your life! You might think, "Well, Eric, there are a lot of aspects of my life that are not enjoyable!"

That might be true; however, He is with you in them all and thereby provides joy *through* it all! The scriptures say, "Therefore God, your God, has anointed you. With the oil of gladness above your companions" (Hebrews 1:9). In other words, there wasn't another man as joyful as Jesus.

Some might say, "Well, sure, but that was for Jesus... not us." Then we must look at another scripture in which Jesus said, "These things I have spoken to you so that **my joy may be in you**, and *that* your joy may be made full" (John 15:11, emphasis added). The joy of Jesus is sharable.

"You have put gladness in my heart" (Psalm 4:7). See, God places joy within us. It's His heart in us. Martin Luther once wrote, "I know how easily one can forfeit the joy of the gospel." It's quite easy to forget how joyful this life really is! We've failed to remember that in the midst of everything, we can experience joy unspeakable by drinking of Him. I don't share these things to tickle ears or to give a shallow encouragement.

I share the message of joy with a deep-rooted conviction that God is going to break joy open over us in a much needed way. It will change everything about our lives! Joy isn't just an idea, but an actual, tangible fruit of God's Spirit!

"In your presence is fullness of joy..." (Psalm 16:11). What does fullness of joy mean? It means there is no area that isn't touched with joy. Mother Teresa once said, "A joyful face preaches without preaching."

I think often we disqualify ourselves when we try to preach the joyful good news of glad tidings without being touched by joy!

How can we preach glad tidings when we ourselves are not glad? When you as a person are dipped into the fullness of God's joy, you will attract people. Folks will want to listen to what you have to say simply because you're smiling so much. If Jesus *really* did die for us and if He *really* did set us free, then an eruption of internal joy can only be the byproduct.

"Restore to me the joy of your salvation" (Psalm

51:12). In other words, the salvation that you have has got joy *sewn* into it. You separate yourselves from the wonderful victories of salvation when you cease drinking of the joy which is Himself. Are you being convinced yet of the happy intention of God?

In the scriptures, *wine* and *joy* are mixed together. "And wine which makes man's heart glad, So that he may make his face glisten with oil" (Psalm 104:15). God literally gifts wine as a gift which is representative of His Spirit. What is the result of drinking of His spirit? Gladness of heart!

Yet it doesn't stop there... He gives reason for this gift: "So that he may make his face glisten with oil." What does it mean to glisten with oil? It's the Spirit of God coming out of your countenance! It's displaying the Person of the Lord. It's bearing His image!

As these things happen and take shape in our lives, we are able to preach without preaching. Of course, we should continue to preach the gospel verbally, without question.

However, with joy on our countenance, there is a preaching that happens in passing someone on the street. Your spouse needs to see a face that's glistening with oil in their lives. Your children need to look up to mom and dad and see a face glistening with oil! Your friends need a friend to look to with a face glistening with oil! This glistening will only happen through joy in the heart which comes from drinking of the Lord.

4

INTOXICATION

Richard Rolle wrote in his book, "When you experience Jesus, He becomes all of your desire, all your delight, all your joy, all your consolation, all your strength, so that your song will always be about Him, and in Him all your rest." He describes a sense of God's presence like this: "a certain sweet gift flows into the pure mind, and, as if drunk with strong wine, she melts completely into the pleasure of the Creator."

He also prayed, "Inebriate my spirit with the burning wine of your sweet love, so that, forgetting all evils and all limited sights, illusions and images, I may exult, embracing you alone, and I may rejoice in God my Jesus."

The intoxication of God causes such joy! It's for you today, it's for you later, it's for you always! I'm simply reminding you of things that you already know! It's not just a holly jolly Christmas, but a holly jolly life!

In Isaiah 9:3 we see that Jesus increases joy, "You have increased their joy." Oh how the church needs an increase of joy. I need it. You need it. Jesus alone can give it. The Psalms give us quite an education in this joy that God gives to men. David writes, "You have put joy in my heart." Psalm 4.7 He goes on to say where His joy comes from and how we can receive.

Joy is in taking refuge in God. Psalm 5:1
Joy is in His presence. Psalm 16:11
Joy is resting in His victory. Psalm 20:5
Joy is connected to righteous living. Psalm 30:11
God is Joy. Psalm 33:1
Joy is in His rule. Psalm 43:14
Joy is in hearing Him. Psalm 48:2
Joy is in repentance. Psalm 51:8,12
Joy is in His shadow. Psalm 63:7
Joy is in His presence. Psalm 84:2
Joy is the Springs of God. Psalm 87:7
Joy is our satisfaction. Psalm 90:14
Joy is in the presence of God, Psalm 95:2

Paul show us that joy is shed abroad in our hearts, by the Holy Spirit. In Romans 15:30 he is telling the Romans that the Holy Spirit burst your heart open with joy. Richard Rolle wrote about this joy in no uncertain terms, "I feel I will die in the face of your joy." Have you ever seen anyone write this way before? He is saying, "I am so joyful that I feel I am going to die." Catherine of Sienna wrote, "I am so filled with joy I am surprised that my soul stays in my body." I am writing this book to tell you that it is for you. It is God's will that you be *animated* with joy in His presence. It is going to come through drinking. I can hear people saying, "Eric, you don't understand, such and such just happened." I say to you, use that situation as another window to pass into God and enjoy Him.

Paul was so convinced of this evidence of the Spirit that he told the Thessalonians that joy is our way of life. (see 1 Thessalonians 5:16) Not some of the time, but "rejoice always." Not just sometimes. All the time. You may say, "Eric, you don't know all the trials going on in my life. James has a good answer for that, "Consider it all joy, my brethren when you encounter various trials" (James 1:2). It is as if he is saying, "In all your trials be joy-filled. See all your trials as an avenue to share in the joy of His presence." In fact, the strength in your trial is tied to the joy you have in it. Nehemiah 8 shows us that joy is our strength. It is the *result* of the Spirit in Galatians 5:22. The work of the Spirit and the gospel in the world is inseparable from "The Spirit of the Lord is upon me, because the Lord has anointed me...to grant those who mourn in Zion, giving them a garland instead of ashes, the oil of joy instead of mourning" (Isaiah 61:1-3).

> *"The strength in your trial is tied to the joy you have in it."*

The presence of God in the person of the Holy Spirit will banish mourning and depression. He will lift the oppression and break the heaviness off of your life and replace it with a lifted heart of joy. Oh many of your hearts are hurting. You feel damaged on the inside because of something you have done, or something someone has done to you. You feel pain inside from weariness and dryness. God does not heal the heart by theology. He heals it by wine. When the New Wine of heaven enters, the old religious wineskins burst! May all the weights fall off of your life as you enter the joy of His presence. May your home be filled with joy. May your marriage be filled with joy. May your relationships be filled with joy... joy of such a kind that even on your way to be martyred, your heart will sing of His unfailing love and beauty.

.

MEET THE AUTHOR

Eric William Gilmour is the founder of *Sonship International*—a ministry seeking to bring the church into a deeper experience of God's presence in their daily lives. He enjoys writing on the revelation of Jesus Christ in the Scriptures and personal experience of God. He lives in Florida with his wife Brooke and their two daughters.

NOTES

Made in the USA
Columbia, SC
21 September 2023